POEMS IN WHICH

Joseph Di Prisco

Winner of the
Dorothy Brunsman Poetry Prize

BEAR STAR PRESS

2000

POEMS IN WHICH © 2000 by Joseph Di Prisco
All Rights Reserved
Printed in the United States of America
by Ed's Printing in Chico, California
10 9 8 7 6 5 4 3 2 1

BEAR STAR PRESS
185 Hollow Oak Drive
Cohasset, CA 95973
www.bearstarpress.com

Cover and author photographs by P. James Fōtōs
Book design by B. Spencer

The typeface used in this book is Garamond. The text
was produced in PageMaker 6.0.

The publisher once again thanks Dorothy Brunsman
for her generous donation of the prize.

ISBN: 0-9657177-5-5
Library of Congress Card Number: 00-190530

ACKNOWLEDGMENTS

Grateful thanks to the editors of the magazines where these poems appeared, sometimes in different form and under different titles:

Blue Unicorn
"Poem in which Orpheus rearranges the world yet again:"
Fine Madness
"Poem in which he often is drowning:"
"Poem in which he has trouble with this elegy for Bathsheba's first husband, Uriah, a loyal soldier whose death in war was neatly arranged by King David, who would become her second:"
"Poem in which appear the special children:"
"Poem in which there is the ultomato, as well as his grandfather, and where he comes close to quoting Gertrude Stein, *Picasso*: 'When he ate a tomato the tomato was not everybody's tomato':"
Kayak
"Poem in which no one appears to show up for his party:"
Midwest Quarterly
"Poem in which he devours a white wolf:"
"Poem in which illustrious Occam shaves:"
Poetry Northwest
"Poem in which he faces a firing squad after weeks of reading Latin American fiction:"
"Poem in which he directs a pretentious, critically acclaimed low-budget movie even though it's obvious he's never even been to film school:"
Poetry Now
"Poem in which he looks past the problems of relationship and forges ahead dreamily:"
Prairie Schooner
"Poem in which we hear the latest news from the Far West:"
Remington Review
"Poem in which an escape takes place:"
Sycamore Review
"Poem in which he demonstrates your influence upon his life:"
"Poem in which he recalls those precious journeys with Wanda:"

Third Coast
"Poem in which the concept of *closure* is addressed:"
Threepenny Review
"Poem in which he depends upon a passing familiarity with
baseball and the works of Sir Walter Scott:"

Thanks especially to those who helped:

Dean Young, poet through whom.

Patricia Ainsworth James. Mario Di Prisco.

J. A. Gray. Marcia Goodman. Hank Combellick. Eric Greenleaf.
Joseph M. Helms. Jack Hazard. Abby, Jack, and Edwina.

to Patti

CONTENTS

Write the vision:
Make it plain on tablets
so that a runner may read it.

Habakkuk 2:2

I got up early Sunday morning
because it occurred to me that the word
which *might have come from a combination*
of who *and* each.

Ron Padgett

I

Poem in which he sets up shop:

How do you *think* the pearl got its start?
First it was shy, loath to forsake a shell so sweet and Polynesian,
and next thing you know, it's a Nieman Marcus frontispiece.
As for me, I've figured out prices but not yet services
I should render. This will come in time, with the first thaw,
with a crate shipped from the Andes or the won ton soup
from downstairs. Things could be tough at first, consider
the competition, which is cut-throat and predacious
and looks a lot like the ex would after sex-change surgery.
I've got to avoid acrimony, which consumers sense.
They catch a whiff of a fire sale and you're dead meat.
Speaking of sex, should I patent that position that makes
them claw at the ceiling in dreams I wish won't stop?
I will accept credit cards, personal checks, scruples,
and splinters off the Holy Rood. My calls may be
monitored for customer satisfaction, their joy is
my number two priority, select the menu that most closely
applies. We can schedule a photo shoot once
I determine what to do with my hands, now that pipes
are passé along with tweed and canonical elbow patches.
Vulnerability can pay off, so let me be caught
cuddling with a banjo or strumming a little llama.
The complications of setting up shop—you have no idea.
I say offer something that can't be done without.
A good matching tong. An explanation of evil. Maps of
a silver mine and a testy caged canary. Stronger lamb, slinkier simile,
thousand-watt testimonial to wilt convention carnations.
I'll get a web site, my own venture capitalist, iron-clad
contracts, and copyright the cassoulet. When I go public
my price-to-earnings ratio will bloom like the wisteria
and off my satellites birds will bounce their psalms.

Poem in which he gives precise directions how to get there:

You'll find it steamy among the courtly Cape Buffalo.
Their conservative political positions are entrenched,
so don't bring up the vegetarianism topic unless
you have time to kill. Now, then, just beyond
the clearing you will enter a restaurant walk-in
refrigerator. A lovely word for what the sun does
going silver is *argentine*. There will be a sign saying
"The Argentine." Go there only if you like
show tunes. Anyway, that's a moat complete with raft.
Paddle, Huck, honey, to the blue island and hunker
down for a good seven years. Write your memoirs,
which are big these days, and wag a magisterial finger.
Master the isle's local tongue. That done,
critique the isms, give to the march of paradigms,
build a mound in the shape of your phallus,
or, if yours is not handy, any available phallus.
Merge with your mother the sea, your sister the moon,
your best friend in high school the weight room.
When you wash ashore, say hello to Nebraska.
Of course, you'll be in Minsk. That's why I'd like,
if I may, to impart some advice I heard that meant
a lot to me when I was refusing to grow up:
Go deep. Move fast. Keep low. Aim high.
(Or was it, Go fast, move deep, aim low, keep high?)
Just pay no attention to harmless harpies. If
you're quiet griffons will gently light on your occiput.
Step carefully around icons, taste indigenous
cornucopias, watch out for shadowy harbingers.
A man will be leaning against a buckeye tree
offering you a kiss. Do what you have to do.
A woman says her breasts are tender, would you stop?
Here's where things get banal: As you drive
through the millennium you'll notice it's quiet

in the hive for this time of night. One more thing,
about the dark thoughts you are beginning to have:
You're almost there. All that's left is to slip on
your headphones and shift into the next worthy gear.

Poem in which no one appears to show up for his party:

The clean-up committee seemed elated,
and so were the old friends who could
never talk heart-to-heart during parties.
Amaryllis and periwinkle, everywhere
birds of paradise, and the not bad
champagne chilled down, and before
I knew it, no one showed. This was good
I guess for someone's grandfather who
post-surgery would have laughed too hard
and the big guy I never would invite
who leaks out tears near the fireplace,
the incredible come-back and drive into
the power pole. At least you-know-who's
husband didn't challenge the whole room
to arm-wrestle and didn't get caught
in the sauna with you-can't-be-serious.
At least what's-her-name (black clunky
shoes, black turtleneck, black garroted hair),
didn't read *The Idiot* sprawled on the love seat.
At least no one fed the Japanese fighting fish
pâté. And no one had the bright idea
of introducing the rottweiler to the toucan.
The whole night, not a whisper of *Tarantino*.
Nice that pillows won't lounge on the lawn,
that no trembling earring washes out to sea.
And good thing the paparazzi will be out of sight
when I turn into the life of my own party
and the wallflower sweeps me off my feet.

Poem in which he shares what he learned today at the spa:

I should take better care of my biggest organ,
says *The Spa News*, and they mean my skin. Were
you aware that you shed 5 billion dead skin cells
a day? That dead skin accounts for 80% of household dust?
If you're anything like me, you won't put off hiring
that domestic help. In the spa I also learned, from
watching the younger smooth organs pass me by,
how to grow old gracelessly. In addition, I have
28 thousand pressure points and 72 channels or so
for chi, and the state of California considers my diet
a class B felony. As I wait here in my plush terry
robe and smart red rubber espadrilles, I would
not dream of telling alien abductors where
to harvest, but here's got to be more fertile
than Roswell, New Mexico. Today I found out, too,
that I do not technically need sex to survive,
though it may in fact need me. Have I mentioned,
not to brag, that my second biggest organ is my
linch pin, my third my thalweg—or is it my lunette?
Did you know that when I am in love my biggest organ
sings, that the air tastes sweet, that your name
is a lozenge down the slide of my throat?
I was all primed for the herbal body wrap (though
it was not rosemary and thyme), and up pops the potpourri
migraine again. Which is when it dawned that I too
will someday die and that deluxe spa packages
would not be ill-advised. No wonder on this slick
of ointment all I want for lunch is extra salt
with my six Margaritas. Pry from my face the cucumber
wedges, let me and my supple nib breathe.

Poem in which he demonstrates your influence upon his life:

I hereby take the city of Chicago and rename it for you.
It was nothing, but you're welcome. Next stop, Minneapolis.
You know, string theory experts, even those ejected from
the ballgame for entering the field of play, opine that six extra
dimensions curl and loop around the staid old ones
we drolly take to the bank—length, depth, breadth,
and miasma. One of these dimensions circulates
you, beyond the bending, the aftershocked echo.
That's where I marvel over the striated sheen of lake
while I'm squinting into the brash matutinal sun.
Remember? How I used to hate change?
Not that kind—coins. Anyway, I'm cooking up a batch
of tender imprinted with the fulgency of your lips.
Keeps me busy till I come up with a name for Cleveland.
Thanks to you, we can cook romantic dinners
using the moonlight concept and works of bereted surrealists.
The phone that's ringing is me wanting to know:
Is that a blue flower in your ear or have I been staring too long?
I can't remember any of my dreams, but I can
recall every detail of yours—including the one in the sidecar
and the scuba gear you donned so fetchingly that I turned
into a tropical fish and navigated between your breasts.
Because of you I plow into woolly snow banks daily,
I laugh at the money in my wallet, I speak
tongues as long as one of them is in your mouth.
I'm singing during my check-up, I'm swinging on—yikes—
your lianas in the rain forest, I'm committing to memory
the transcript of every single one of your previous tears.
I'm planning on crashing any weddings that get in my way
in hopes one will be ours. And because I can't figure out
what else to do with these wings, I'm always almost
ready to take flight off my roof into your arms.

One day I may turn into a cantor and I did not know
I owned a yarmulke. My unread books expose themselves
like exotic dancers, but modest ones, tricky with a feather boa.
Why, only last night a crank caller woke me at midnight
to tell me the true plot of *Twelfth Night*, for which I am
most glad. I am yodeling in subways. I'm moving so fast
I may as well be standing still. See? I'm the one
turning the corner right now, tugging on
the newfound string of the universe that's you.
Later if you need me I'll be working on that poem
in which I demonstrate your influence upon my life.

Poem in which he explains exactly what it is he is working on:

Funding has come through at last, and that's why
everybody here will be busy on the Indolence Project
—just as soon as we wrap up the Oral History of
Disappointment. I think you of all people will appreciate
the difficulties we endured with Principles of Thigmotaxis
Among Declined Love Interests. That's why we postponed
The Sex Life of the Thin-Skinned. There's a downside
to hitting it big when you're young, but was it my fault
I isolated the charisma-chromosome-deficiency
syndrome? That was still the 70s, but my Institute
was soon up and running: Cross-gender Winking Research . . .
Fun with Irony . . . Why This Dog Won't Hunt . . .
It would be great to feel the support of colleagues
like you once more, or at least if you would please
stop making a racket running the court upstairs.
If someone with your vision would consider taking
a seat on the Board we would find the collective will
to pursue Post-(P)sumo Wrestling, Tequila and I Forget,
Gnome on the Range & other Punnic Victories,
Strategies of Linguistic Enforcement: High School
Handbooks and the Rates of Recidivism in
Catcher in the Rye. We would stay on task,
be on point, break up into small groups and confer,
put our noses to the grindstone, our bodies to whipped
cream. (Where *did* you put the red shantung teddy?)
All day, the molecules chant like tonsured monks
and I knock down doors for words hiding inside.
Lately, the words have been *carapace*,
louche, and *rupestral*, but I'd like to report
progress on my new proposal for *ravishment*.

Poem in which he goes to the exhibit, where he is ambushed:

If I never see another portrait
of the mild Virgin, one more tumescent nymph,
or a triptych of death and the sacred cross.
If I never see you in your midnight bath.
If I never see a ship ablaze,
if I never see rollicking peasants,
their elliptical loaves or their unworkable wooden shoes,
or wiseguy gargoyles or slouchy burghers in floppy hats.
Let me see you with a sketch pad
in, let's say, autumn. If I never see the screech of
lines, tweaked cornfields, or a bandaged ear,
a girl reading or petting a little white dog,
if I never see the mismatched landscape
on either side of her misaligned face.
Spare me the stag that is tragically slain,
the dismounting king, the strife in the sunset,
spare me the sight of you on that landing.
Spare me dark woods in the mid-afternoon,
shadows cool as blades on the back of my neck,
the bird's cry yanking open my eyes,
the rustling in the brake and the crackling of twigs.
Spare me a summer you never returned.
See if I don't notice the delicate interplay of
light and dark, see if I don't stand in line to admire
the emperor's sarcophagus, see if I don't return
the look you give me touring the Vermeers.

Poem in which he is a lion, including some wasted hours in Paris:

Once I was a hedgehog but now I like
being a lion. Most of your aardvarks
caught on videotape will stipulate as much.
I have been known to be an ocelot,
but I think it's pretty obvious I am a lion.
Like all teenagers, I went through the phases:
possum, stingray, vampire, bison, regret.
I mean egret. Because I am now a lion
I don't worry about strangers circling my nest
anymore and can't be bothered to crawl in
my shell for the hike down to the eggy shore.
Of course, when I was a marlin I dreamed
I was a stallion and when I was a stallion
I dreamed I was singing like a meadowlark.
Once I swooped like a bluejay chockachawing!
and sampled like a giraffe the topmost leaves.
It was too much responsibility to timberwolf
around, to eagle upon the craggy heights.
Now time is a wormwood blur and I speak
impeccable French, a perfect lion. Maurice and Charles
present me the special menu, they light my unfiltered
cigarettes, they decant my wine through candlelight.
As I say, I am a lion. Sometimes I miss polar bear
when I wait in the parched clearing, for being
a lion is not all complex protein and carnivore games.
Everyone wants a piece, and when you walk in
the gallery you don't know what to look for,
or even how to look yourself, you are a lion.
When you write letters home, you start,
"Dear X, I'm sick to death in love with you
& I'm in Paris and X is not your name &
I'm sizing up a post-Cubist portrait by somebody

you have probably also slept with baroquely..."
The rooftops of Paris gleam with golden darts
—I think it must have rained since I was last out.
Then at the artist's reception I talk with somebody
who has skidding tire tracks for eyes. There are
bodies in the cellars, I admit to a sense of relief
you are in LA, that I don't have my own cri de coeur
or compensation package, I don't tell her
Sidney is my first name as well as my last. Success
I attribute to the excellence of my personal contacts
gleaned during those formative undergraduate years,
long before I was a lion. Do you like being watched
bathing in the river among other gazelles?
"Do you think a lion like me has a chance?"
"For what," she says, and tilts her champagne flute.
"And besides, remarks are not literature, but Sweet Jesus
you could try." Tomorrow I could end up an elephant,
I swear. My ears would fan the veld, my trunk
would swing like a philosopher armed with tenor sax.
Till then, I am a lion and I yawn in the teeth of the sun.

Poem in which he is sick with love:

If you find my beloved, say I am faint with love.
Say I am sick with love.

Song of Solomon 5:8

Then say, right after, I'm sorry
about the former goldfish, the posthumous automobile,
the previous wisteria trimmed during the cherry cough
syrup sundae scenario. Say, before she steps on the gas,
I'll never preach to her again from a farther room.
Then say, she *did* look like a million bucks
in her new color, her new dress, her new do,
her new certification from the Institute. If you find
my beloved, ask her, does she need me to pick up
the dry cleaning, the shoe repair, or how about
the spring rolls and won ton soup she phoned in?
Convince her I've had a good month or two
at work—without any sort of serious incident.
Tell her. Tell her *three.* Ask her how things go
with the new therapist—and tell her I regret
I did not make the appointment that time.
Is her trainer still Lance? Lance LaFlame? He seems
committed to her overall personal self-realization.
Tell her Snowy is checking for messages twice a day,
and that I don't seem to be allergic to Snowy as
I used to be. Tell her I've waxed her pus-yellow Saab,
tuned it, and mounted four new replacement tires.
She'll know what I mean. *If you find my beloved,*
tell her I have established relations with my inner
Cro-Magnon, my outer orangutan, my median math score...
Look, just tell her, all right.
Is she seeing somebody else these days? What's his name?
Are the turkey leftovers still good to eat? And is she
aware of how much she owns fast approaches
the date of expiration? You can tell her, if you like,
I am finally picking up the subjunctive mood,

and finding everyday use for handy conditions which
are contrary, really fucking contrary to fucking fact.
Let her think I have reversed positions on
punishment capital, hockey ice, mother her.
Speaking of wine, tell her I have cellared a dozen
cases of the 90s, which I would love to sample
in the cool solemn darkness underground
with a tasty chevre, like her, any day.
Ask her if she's taking what I gave her for the pain,
something for that pinched nerve in her arm?
Find out if she saw the new moon last night over
the laminations of the bay out by San Quentin.
Remind her, I have sold the Vette, the blues tapes,
the gun, the boombox, and the leather bomber.
Say I was wrong about rap and about Bill Clinton,
wrong about the way the sun bounced off her eyes
that time on Mount Tam and everything I screamed
before lunch on the bike path when she slipped
and a cut bisected the perfect circle of her left
cheek. Tell her I've left all the album pages
blank, in case she brings the black and whites home.
Only, find my beloved. You know I am sick in love.
Plead for her number, beg if you have to for
the first letter of her name. Is that a G, like in Gretchen?
                                        It is Gretchen?
I knew no way it was going to be Imogene.

Poem in which he delivers the keynote address to the daily convention of those he let down:

Innocent bystanders and cathected guests. Flouncy and admonished
former flames. Once-upon-a-time not-insignificant others. Other
others. Professors and piano instructors. Coaches. Students
still hoping for letters of recommendation or final grades.
A special welcome to parents and family, especially
deceased. Please keep your admission stubs. First prize
in the drawing: solo dining at the half-star Obloquy Cafe.
Word is they work wonders with a suckling pig.
Something tells me lay off the lamb shanks, though.

So thank you for taking time out from your busy schedule
haunting my dreams. Can you hear up there in the cheap seats?
Good. This thing is on. Heartfelt thanks go out to participants
in this morning's panel sessions: "Snap Out of It."
"What Do You Mean, You Forgot?" "Seemed to Be
the Thing to Do at the Time." Would my offspring
please stand and take a bow? Just a thought, never mind.

I'd like to announce that I have finally unearthed
those missing opera tickets, and the aeolian harp,
and the metaphor for the old apple tree outside my window
that figures so prominently in several key unfinished works.
I'd like to add, too, that I now can lift my bat off
my shoulder and swing at that dubiously called strike three.
The search party I sent out is making solid progress on
the wedding album, the urns of dust and charred bone,
the satchel of love letters never quite sent soon enough.

In the little time I have left, I'd like to thank my friends
for sending me your books. I have figured out the software.
To my enemies who sent me your books, if you camp out
at the mailbox waiting, pack a hearty lunch. As for the Buick

Skylark, Percy, did you get the bouquet? I had no idea about
the tires. How could I know the soothsayer would not take
a personal check? Rupert, my best dog, I did all I could
for you in the end, and it was not enough to keep
your eyes from going flat as a camera lens. The plaid suitcase,
Marv, I did not know that's where you kept your best ideas
or that the new girlfriend would not find palatable my
hot tub reference. Hazaiah, I missed that moment
they broke into song and you strolled up to Jesus
and the sporting sun leaped like a marlin onto the hospital floor.

Finally, though, I've been sensing a little groundswell building
on behalf of the redevelopment project named Forgive Myself.
In that spirit, please reach under your chairs, go ahead.
Don those party hats and slip on your dancing shoes.
Any second Veuve Cliquot will come to a nearby glass.
Death, you see, is the lurking one in black tie and cummerbund,
dressed for the ball that coincides with the end of this event
called my life. He's not as tough as he seems, or was, or maybe is.
And trust me, there's nothing he can try anymore
that the expiatory rain hasn't already absolved.

Poem in which he often is drowning:

Often while he is drowning in a particular summer lake
John Fitzgerald Kennedy is the first President
who's Catholic of, of course, the United States.

They say this—about Kennedy—as if choirs of Catholics,
heads bowed, wait in line, solemn communicants,
to take the next oath of office alongside that Protestant

Robert Frost, whose woods, memorized in class, are lovely
—lovely, dark, and deep. But is anything as deep as this
drowning, as dark as the bottom of this lake?

So, often as he feels himself dying in early June,
in New Jersey, he has just turned ten in God's pure love,
and when he drowns he goes into a smoked green glass

bottle. He pushes against the heavy sides and feels
the closing in, and the utter impossibility of clouds
in a presumable sky that carried Jesus, then Mary,

his mother, for a while away. Still, it's beautiful
almost down here. The trailing bubbles of expended air
remind him of the circles on the standardized answer sheet

for a vocational aptitude test that he filled in neatly
with his Number Two sharpened lead pencil, which
he did not forget to bring to school. Come to think of it,

there wasn't one single thing he ever forgot to bring
to school. Still, drowning is not much of a career move.
Or is it? Certainly, nothing like second Catholic President

of the United States. Nothing like Father Paul, Duke Snider,
Jimmy the Weasel, all the celebrities he ever knew.
But now he breaks out of the airtight bottle and

tumbles around like the stars, like science project molecules,
and the water is cold and heavy as mercury, and hitting bottom,
he kneads a few last desperate sculptures made of clay.

Below the surface, in the darkening deep, is where
he was always meant to be. These are the currents
he has always waited for, and his head fills up

with water and a true prayer. So he grows calm,
and begs God not to save him. To let him come
back to where he has always belonged.

Everything goes soft and black, like a hood
drawn down on his head, the equivalent of grace, of sleep,
the gentleness of things unknown, sweetness always to be

unperceived, moments never to savor or endure.
And it is perfect, drowning in this particular summer lake.
All the snapshots fade to black in their frames.

All the big decisions unravel, mistakes unmade.
All the lost hours reclaimed, lost lovers redeemed.
Give up the future for the prospect of eternity.

But it crosses his mind: perhaps these are Satan's real works
and his emptiest promises—to imagine a world without him,
a blank book, a bare canvas, an erasure, an eclipse.

—How it might have all been different, if someone else
had taken his place... forgotten the names of the people...
driven to the wrong destination... somehow said the wrong
words—

Yet every time he is drowning in a particular summer lake,
a man is pulling him back up to the stifling air,
throwing his body with the certainty of heaven

onto the mud of shore. Just like that, thirty years
go by, shadows of flight on a summer lake, undoing of time,
and still he wonders how surviving could be
what it possibly means to be blessed.

II

Poem in which he recalls those precious journeys with Wanda:

Wanda, we traveled from Pigs-in-Sunny-Abattoir, Hungary,
to Tourist-Train-Ambushed-Magic-Midnight, Mozambique,
from Fighter-Pilot-Dying-at-Dawn, Afghanistan,
to Bird-of-Paradise-Gash-Gold-Vermilion, Ring of Fire.
Such a tiny, combustible, fractious planet, don't you think?
We bought a thousand postcards and took snaps of the syllogisms.

My cherished Wanda, I still can't get through my head
how you managed to speak, wherever we went,
in the local patois. Was it in Pakistan or Peru you ventured,
in perfect idiom, "My feet take two steps before I do,"
and they rose and cheered and picked up our check?
Where is there now left for me, dearest Wanda, to go?

True, once, a very lonely night, we fell in love, though
I attribute that one indiscretion to the influence
of the sun's pouring through the stained glass epic tale
of martyrs, wisemen, and the babe in swaddling clothes.
We share a weakness for reliquaries and acedia.
And the cathedral crushed us, that and the grappa flask.

I still see you on every empty platform, in shadows
of flight, in the fast-changing weathers. I still seek you out
in the back of planes, in cafes, on all the crowded streets.
Recall when once we came upon a weeping schoolgirl
near a fountain in Rome? We took to the hotel for a week.
Now, the leopards enfilade the gusting savannah
and my lungs are ventilated by your blood.

Poem in which he looks to find his voice:

I decompensated the galleria shopkeeper,
ladling out 17 billion lire, one by one,
a bargain for a first-edition blazing bonfire.
But in the split second while I admired those
perfect teeth of hers and tried to put the past
behind me, and the busted transmission and cracked
daguerreotypes, I was momentarily entranced
by those mordacious green eyes, slightly carnal,
and just like that when I turned back to where
I thought my voice was handy, it was gone.

I searched but it did not lurk among fluorocarbons,
wasn't lounging inside the socks drawer, wasn't
growling with the other joists after the temblor.
I sought it out amidst the yowls at the pound,
the speckled one with cocked ear had me going.
It wasn't in the jar of cold coins, it wasn't stuck
on the windshield, it wasn't tap-dancing in the shoe
mausoleum. I cracked the spines of my seven books,
soaked off the wine labels, combed the factotum's
hair. Underneath the eggs in the nest abandoned,
stripping off dry wall tape, snapping with laundry
on a windy clothesline, south of central semaphore,
north of the hierophants. Tub filling with beer,
the rustling alarum of a rabbi's beard, plaid skirt
of a school girl, tugging on a turkey wishbone,
hoping world peace, engine turned over, dust on a road,
guitar pick and sickle, swoop of a raven wing,
refrigerator hum, snap of finger, slap of face,
butane shush, wheelchair hum, rosepetal scoop
over corporal nakedness, which was my default dream setting,
and much more compact than my gamma-ray burster.

My vermilion flyers fluttered on martial telephone poles.
For a long time after I'd slow down at the corners,
parts of town where other voices go to get right.
I resolved if ever I got my voice back
I would not lend it out or let it run loose again.
Once I heard someone telling a few whoppers
at a Beverly Hills party and I thought for a second:
that could be my voice. I recognized the twang,
the tinny majorettes at the grand parade. Thus I was
unsurprised when the kidnappers' note appeared.
They wanted a ransom of two rainbows and the environs
of Seattle. A small price to pay, I knew,
so I threw in the Green Bay Packers and my rewrite
of *Wuthering Heights*, a less comic update, if you will.
It was worth it, every penny, every radiance, each
raindrop and mocha latte, when I saw my voice
step off the biplane and trip across the tarmac
toward my feathery arms. So much to catch up on,
ground to cover, tattoos to send out for bleaching.
Tell me what's with the accent, which I still can't place.

Poem in which we hear the latest news from the Far West:

For love he would squeeze her a thousand oranges
if she wanted them, would lurk through the dark hours
outside and scavenge in the hen house for the fresh
green and speckled eggs at dawn.
He would pound out the loaves of bread
at the bakery or deliver the milk or the morning
paper in the big white truck. If she wished.
Or he would make her coffee black and strong
the way he liked it, or let her tea steep and then
slightly cool. He'd knock down a tree for
the honey and ladle it into her wordless mouth.
If he was just crazy, why would he return,
what use would he have for a gun,
for the ax, for the maps of the trails, for
the magazines they'd soon put her prom picture in?

Poem in which while judging a spelling bee he has a minor breakdown over "argillaceous":

Contestants palpitate on the grade-school
stage, and their dental appliances shimmer
like quaking aspen in the coltish breeze.
Roots and stems bulge in their pockets,
backpacks jammed with Greek, Latin, Sanskrit,
and cheese. Silent P acts like a psychopath,
silent B, a lot like a lamb on a limb.

A sibyl tells sibilant anecdotes in the pharmacy, too,
and diachronic ecdysiast is a shibboleth to them,
who gallivant with any lepidopterist
while ichthyologists converge.
The contestants are not dyspeptic,
though one stumbles on the sentinel's armamentarium
and another chokes down a cicerone with a macaronic.
No, this oeuvre is batrachian as a swamp,
and no chatelaine is safe, no satrap, podesta, or paladin.
Put on your plenipotentiary's swaddling clothes
reeking of frankincense, parsimony, and myrrh!

"Can you use that word in a sentence please?"
He locates the notecard and reads into the mike.
Giddy with quotidian antibiotics,
he lopes across the argillaceous ground.
Which of course is way too pellucid to live.

The judge wonders why it is he can't spell.
He pulls out the CAT scan and discreetly examines
his cerebral cortex. There on the brain map where
words go to be spelled a For Sale sign towers in
a vacant lot advertising COMMITMENT, while
a rat which lives in SEPARATE forages in grey dark.

So rises he unshod and interprets *argillaceous*
as if he's Martha Graham, and graphs it on a handy x/y axis,
and stretches his canvas, swabbing it twelve colors of mood.
He'd been invited to rip off the words' bandages
but he didn't think he'd irrigate the origin of wounds.

Poem in which he devours the white wolf:

I noticed the climate in the fairy tales
had suffered a change, and musty discolorations

of pages turned amber, and slowly
the sky filled with illegible migrations,

which are the accounts of childhood. So when the day
turned porcelain, stainless steel, and white tile,

windowless fluorescence and high ceilings, my eyes
smarting from the glint on the tables that were

loaded down with a hundred surgical knives of
divers lengths and purposes, I felt in a manner of speaking

prepared. That moment, it all changed, into trivial sunlight,
and small romantic tables, postcard hotels and bistros,

bottles of wine translating the brightness,
an enormous prism in the doorway catching it all,

letting the purple, the gold, the red and blue sadness
stain the walls. And then day just kept turning

over and over, fast, from book to hospital to hotel,
from harbor, to vineyard, to cemetery,

from roads home to roads out of town,
from robbery of the grave, to Mass, to lovemaking,

all the way to the high flat country I never knew
and the cellars of my house swimming with storied rats,

teachers with apples and federal agents,
husbands and their wives, anthropologists,

ones thinking music, doing calculus, ones
discussing string theory for hours over canapés.

That's only a fire examining my house.
You know from the drills how you're supposed

to touch a door first before you open.
If it's hot, you should stay put.

What if the door is always hot?

Poem in which appear the special children:

Tonight, if not everywhere, special children restless
are, are in their cribs, parents arriving unto them
while buoyant their heads arrhythmical kiss
the slick red spongy big bars of the bed.

So, and so, special children turn quiet
in their littler rooms, start to otherwise
laughing on dirty jokes the shoes are telling,
the shattering stars, the shit in their golden pants.

Sometimes, you know, getting angry are these,
the special children, with swooping down phones,
and coffee cups that must spill up, sometimes
new pictures need to be cracked open on the walls.

Special children are being thought of
running, and all go falling down in lonely malls.
From the corners of the mouths they're only bleeding.
Their slow eyes slide when they cry to the sleeping.

Can they be now sleeping? Just, please be sleeping?

Poem in which he catalogues instances of touch:

The nimbus of a basketball's nub.
Two of your most precious toes.
The snout of a stand-up comic crocodile.
But breasts, now, they lead the pack.
The soft pointy ear of a mouse, misfortunately.
The coat of a white whippet named Edwina.
A caftan embroidered with a thousand tea roses.
A stack of Ben Franklins on a felt table.
The bronze handle of the casket.
The score for *West Side Story* dancing
off the piano in the wind storm.
But let's not lose contact with breasts.
Your hair, falling on my face, next pillow.
That pillow, recovered after being lost
all night and on its own, but now held close
and cool to my chest, which made me
sleep through the alarm and the interview
with Allied Mythmakers, "full-service agents
to the stars." The stars. I didn't know they could
be touched but now they flutter in my grasp
like the wings of a moth I can't quite coax
away from the lamp, even when I carry it
tickling my palms to the door and
I have to turn off the lamp and sit
in darkness gone ridged as corduroy.
The darkness: sometimes the brush
of an echolocating misunderstood mammal
crucial to the ecology of the world where we live.
Sometimes a 2 X 4 or the plumage of a macaw.

**Poem in which he, despite being historically the
sort of student who falls in love with his teachers,
struggles with foreign language acquisition:**

So you can't roll your R's, can't trill your L's,
and you can't cluck a Q to save your life.
Still, Study In Your Spare Time CDs
constantly chirr in your pachydermatous ear.
But when you ask the concierge for a room with bath
all you manage to express is a wish to attend
the Piltdown Man Show at high noon.
So much you intend is lost in translation's blitz.
I refer to the time the florist went blank
when you remarked on her crazy escutcheon.
And what did you expect the gendarme to do
when you told him that you required
the services of a radiant neurosurgeon?
And then at the super-realist's benefit bash
you apologized for losing your head in a fuggish canoe.

Run your tongue on the braille of the other's world.
Brush up on verbs of betrayal and ennui.
Forget nouns, carry pronouns in a sack
tied with a string of exclamation points.
Pick a fight, if you must, with a *slow* ontologist.
Do not pass up any opportunity to
disarm a bomb in a revolutionist's gym bag.
Before long you will be conversing with whales,
the parrot will come around to your point of view,
and you will lope alongside the family dog
tracking the silent whistle's commensal source.
Learn the right gifts to break a heart,
when to order one more shot than you can use,
how to get a beauty's attention on the strand
while you're surfing the riptide.

How to dress the lines for the blizzard that's due,
how to ululate till a clerk's brain seizes
and you can steal the sunglasses of your dreams.
One day, your regrets will sleep upside down
like bats in the vowels. For now, let's familiarly address
the sun and let's inscribe red X's on names you use for love.
If you want to take her breath away though
just make your lips do this.

Poem in which he looks past the problems of relationship and forges ahead dreamily:

I said it was like falling asleep nowhere
and waking in some beautiful new country
and if I can get a visa I want to inhabit you
like the beautiful country you are
on the long continent of the late afternoon
in the middle of the season of nothing else is
where the phone never rings again or just once more
a reminder of everything else taking place everywhere else

In a minute I will distribute the glossy blue postcards
and tack this poster up on the wall
with diamond studs from your ears
Here are the local instructions about local customs
local water local food and festivals
so you will know precisely
what I do not mean

There may be birds but nothing as indifferent
as condors or eagles or swans
and all you know and I will know
(I can't keep you out of this)
is how the trees keep shedding music
at, say, four o'clock. *Say, Four o'clock* . . .
by which I mean to say right now

brushing aside the possibility of insurrection
the political independence of this tropical paradise
the question of the rainy season coming on
and the problem of the rainy season coming on

Poem in which "To think at this late date . . .":

. . . we bolt upright from bed in a cold sweat
fearful we, have misplaced a comma.

Later we check to see our socks match
and if it's time to resuscitate the couplets.

To think, we consume fossil fuel to rush across
town to catch the dinosaur symposium.

At this late date, so much at this late date.
We charm, we please, we scrape, we mewl, we carp

around buffets, backstage, the cruise, I am
bic pentameter, to think this is called for anymore.

That we sleep on sheets, that we still cook the meat,
that we're impressed by the rouged dossier of

her cheeks, to think at this late date we compose
our most challenging work thus far.

That this is the path to the waterfall, that the sound
the sky makes is the applause of a thousand wings,

that the clearing is anything but and the white
light in the harbor still guides us along

at this late date, to think I almost never knew you,
that we stroll vanquished into the squawk and squeal,

the hum and whoosh of the woods, to think at this late date
we want to know how we and the poems will end.

III

Poem in which he attempts an answer to Pablo Neruda's question—"In the end won't death be an endless kitchen?":

Hey, that's my *mother's* endless kitchen!
The fierce whiteness of eggs,
the bread that sighs in our hands.
So much cinnamon dust we can't stop
laughing, my brother and I. Baskets
of apples, red bell peppers, tomatoes,
mounds of brown sugar and saharas of salt,
parma hanging like an ampersand on a hook.
Garlands of rosemary, parsley, and basil.

(Speaking of Neruda, I once walked around
his Isla Negra home, and he owned lots of things
for a Marxist, including dolls, hats, guns, masks,
and one papier-mâché stallion. He also set up
his bar on a boat docked in a flagstone courtyard
elevated a hundred yards from shore)

To return to death, I would argue with Neruda
about nothing, but in my mother's endless kitchen,
she is always storming: "Who let the jaguar in again!"

The sun is blocked by a cloud of confections
and sapiential grapes stock the book shelves.
I've never once used the word "tranquil"
without paying for it, so I won't point up
how the sea shakes and leaps like fire
when we blow the candles out, when we let
the meandering stars stream inside.

Tonight, Neruda, my mother's singing
her one aria, she who could never carry a tune.
We have a notable absence of fens in here

and dragons foraging among the bones.
Tonight, even I can write the saddest lines
while she is liminally framed, ascending her stairs,
going up always where endlessness begins.
So we'll wash our dishes till sunup
and listen for the music from her forest of spoons.

Poem in which he is driving westward and it's Good Friday:

Need a God by whom electroconvulsive
therapy would be contraindicated of me.
Need a God to walk with me alongside
The Serotonin Reuptake Blockered
Happy People, need a God, I think.
Need a God, to struggle with me,
cast me down, snap a good rib of me,
need, OK *need*, a God.
Need a God to raze the whole house of me,
torch fields, books, flood the cellars of me,
as I think I've implied, need a God.
Need a plan, need some sleep, need a God,
need rain, need sun, need idea, need a God.
Need a God to help me select with
my non exist slash high-paid decorator "Margot"
chic blackout blinds for me,
contemplate otherwise balanced breakfast for me.
Need a God to go over with me
news re: friends, loss of. Need a God
to help keep track, need a God
to wake me with slap, need a God
to lift me, not drop me down to tiled,
mosaic floor. Help me in muck,
in mire, the bog, on mountain making
those shadows over me, or bottom of the lake,
in friendly convenient all-night liquor
stores, a God's name on my lips, a God
whose name is always on my lips. God, need
new voice, new words, God, to get this rock
off the chest of me, God,
take ice cube out of the mouth of me.
Take the wheel, go on, you can.
And play music you like, go ahead.

Just play. We'll make this our little ritual.
Our uniforms come ripped from the stars.
And right here, at the curve, I'll stop
so you can see Asia if you want.
See the sea shining black like flanks of a horse?
Later, all right? I wish you'd please drive.
Seems like it's not my car.

Poem in which he is harangued by the minor Old Testament prophet Habakkuk, about whom, conveniently, nothing is known:

Just don't count on this being the night you pen
"One could do worse than be a swinger of birches."
And that's not neuralgia coming on—it's me
banging the pizza-sized tambourine in your ear.
You think I'm impressed you're sleeping with
half the girls calling themselves Colette in New York?
I don't care that you're big and heartless in the city,
that you juggle three pugs, that you have a plot
of fictional purple tulips, that you know how
to work the vodka, the moon, and a straight razor.

My wrath is like a river. My God, why do the righteous
suffer? Why do the evil laugh at every fortress?
I'm going to stand at my runic watchpost
and raise my tablets when you run by in your darkness.
For I may be a minor prophet but I do know you:
The time you flung your sandals from the rope bridge
into the gorge, and the Thai girl Meow in Phuket
where kick-boxers' sweat landed in your Singha.
She seemed to read what was left of your mind,
later washed her platinum hair in your sink.
This is the night I put everything else in. This is flying
home. This is song. This, the house in flames.
This is the night you lick the girl's soles till she screams.
You have not been yourself since the crows
decided on your garden, since that, you know, war.
Your test results are back. Am taking a look at your book.

Poem in which he explains how you may best prepare for reading *The Brothers Karamozov*:

I would practice your spitting and sputtering from
stupendous heights. I would cultivate a healthy respect
for testamentary salvoes ventured from the ice floes.
I would not personally tango with a bear I was not
already acquainted with. I would contemplate rumors
spread by a quorum of dysfunctional lynxes.
I would pray—and to God, too. I'd lift outsized
Chinese chests if they were painted orange or red,
consume the contents of the nearest carp pond.
I'd reorganize the address book and resolve never
to lose another phone number. I would find an excuse
to stick around for the conclusion of a conversation
that begins *The night is a shield I have plundered!*
But I belabor the obvious, all of you kneeling in stained
cassocks are too polite to point up. Nobody is
polite in *The Brothers K,* which fact is refreshing as gelid
frozen vodka before you meet your one o'clock World
Lit class at one-twenty-five. I would not celebrate the rosy
cheeks of any nubile creature unless I meant
business. I would always mean business even if I had
no business to mean. I would save my stray kopeks,
I would introduce myself to the Orthodox Icons,
I would not trim my beard on the Sabbath, I would
not kidnap the progeny of any Czar or Czarina.
I'd learn, if I had to, Russian. I would submit early
my request to be reborn in Petersburg. Then let's you
and me challenge the first rake of a cavalry captain
we come across to a duel. He's smacked our fathers
with the heel of his glove, he's plowed our fields under,
he's seduced our sisters and stolen the family diadem.
Later we break into houses and drown the parched plants.

Poem in which there is the ultomato, as well as his grandfather, and where he comes close to quoting Gertrude Stein, *Picasso:* "When he ate a tomato the tomato was not everybody's tomato ":

My grandfather grew those tomatoes.
Pasquale grew tons of tomatoes
and tied my father to a post in the cellar
when he was bad and beat him
in the dark. The world. It is starving
and his children are stuffed with his tomatoes.

When my grandfather ate a tomato
his tomato was not anyone else's tomato.

In the rows of vegetables, zucchini,
broccoli, and corn, painted on my canvas,
rows of eggplant, basil, and tomato,
I find rabbit pellets and silvery tracks of
snails assuming cubist formations.

I recall Pasquale in the kitchen,
eating a tomato while the whole house reeks
of vinegar, olive oil, and red peppers,
while the chicken spatters in the hot pan,
and I can still see—

my grandfather bowing his head on Sunday
at Our Lady of Perpetual Pomodoro Church
as Father Rosario raises his hands to heaven,
his vestments embroidered with vines.

Poem in which he considers indifference at midnight (after a line by Philippe Soupault, "Comme l'indifférence est belle à minuit"):

Indifferent at seven-forty-five, or dawn, that I get.
But used to be, come midnight you would catch me
going, "That's a fascinating brooch you've broached,
tell me more about your animadversions!" Or, "Sure,
we've got plenty of gas to get to the summit," or,
"Hey, let's do that one again, but first how about
a bite of your little madeleine?" Cute, perhaps fetching,
possibly oleaginous, but beautiful? I would have
kept that one in reserve. No more though.
Beauty, rubicund wonder, be my midnight now.
Lethargy is passé, remoteness, de rigueur.
Dénouement, éminence grise, fait accompli,
ménage à tuna—there, I've used up most of
French One. Oh, and décolletage, a favorite.
Midnight was the time to start your paper on
"Heart of Darkness. Cardiac Arrest?"
That's when you banged out the Bangor File,
when you hammered out terms for
the Hammerman Account. You catch a game,
you order onions on the burger and care less,
you tell the guy on the Harley to move his piece
of crap. Later, you walk the floors midnight
with your child in your arms, waiting for
ampicillin to kick in, hoping your own crepitant
melodies can salt him into sleep.
My Beautiful Midnight Indifference.
Well, it is a relief from midnight desiring,
rambling, scouring, seizing, sneezing.
Those are lovely handles it has, that's velvet
lining the cedar box, we've got hours till

morning and nobody I can see's laughing.
I think I'll always miss, though, the frisson
of a shooting star and the busted tail light
entrée to those who would serve and protect
our community from people like me.
So what if I can't promise always to be
indifferent at midnight? I'm committed still
to my rowdy nap in the trope of the afternoon

Poem in which he directs a pretentious, critically acclaimed low-budget movie and it's obvious he's never even been to film school:

Golden carriages arrive   *pulled by black horses*

We have lived our lives in this hard steady rain
One day it seems to abate   but this calm
becomes an aspect of the storm   this silence
is luminous a moment   Inside of me the horses breathe
The trees take root in the lungs
The curtains exhale   and just by holding to
this ledge   just by looking out there
and under the colonnade   in my white suit
the stairway crawls down to you   I desiderate
into a language I cannot control   more inflected
my God than Greek   My words become steps and
on the edge of my tongue you trip and fall
into the opening ground   we speak   in another tongue
In the movie   you and I lose what remains of our lives

Yellow carriages arrive   *pulled by red horses*

Of course we have the man with a blue patch over
his left eye   Unceremoniously he shoots the chandelier
The tapestry is set aflame   The anchorite wanders off
into the wood   the carved railings take him in
chandelier falling   the complex music   splintering
absolute tonality   Nature is defeated   No cry
of a pathetic songbird needs to be compared
and the translucent voice   the spectral song
This man with a blue eyepatch takes dead aim at
the sky and misses everything   draws a bead on
the ground and fires into the heart of the sun
Until the next frame   Yes, the perfect crime

Green carriages arrive　　　　*pulled by blue horses*

My gradual eyes focus on the distance which is
an oak tree　　　　　　　　and the red clouds frame it against
the hills　　　　Cut away　　　Pick up the birds of prey
circling　　　　　Cut to the clouds swelling on the horizon
Now cut to the white wolves silent in the arms
of the tree　　　　They have come for me I know
I am miserably equipped with my disguises
as I walk through my part as the rain on the lake
as the drowning in the lake　　as the boat loosely moored
as the glass shattering on the floor　　as the fire
kindled in the grate　　everywhere as cloud chandelier curtain
Cut back to
white carriages drawn by white wolves
white wolves driving white carriages

Poem in which illustrious Occam shaves:

That spare, angular Occam.
He stropped his razor sharp and clean
and eliminated

uncertain speculations about
reality. He'd spent his working day
trimming overgrown

hedges wherever he found them.
So he left his razor in
the toilet streaked

with stale lather and black stubble.
This bitter, lonely Occam.
So I took up that same razor.

And then it was no longer April
with rose petals drifting in
the breeze, no soft raining,

it was just you sitting across
the room. I was not still
as water looking on you,

only nervous, your voice would not
pass for mandolin, your eyes jade,
your hair the long wheat fields.

That failed man. You were your interpretation.
I put his razor back,
regard the mere clouds,
pursue the black dragons.

Poem in which he considers plagiarizing a poem by Robert Desnos (1900-1945), you know, the one that, translated, begins, "There is a precise moment of time / When a man reaches the exact center of his life":

I was screaming at my Muse, it was 3 AM,
she looked like shit, and what made her
think she was my Muse anyway, hanging out
at biker bars, the MLA, pouring my troubles into
others' ears, giving away my ideas for poems
as if poems had ideas, some kind of Muse,
I used to count on her, I used to please her,
take her where she told me to go. Now, I can't
stand hearing about her former liaisons,
Mistress Bradstreet, Browning, George Herbert,
the list goes on. As if I care, I mean, why
can't she tell this is the middle of my life?
Doesn't she know the signs? I'm writing
sestinas, I'm organizing the postcards for
the lucky college archive yet to be named.
Must I remind her about the terminal disease?
Must I make a fool of myself yet again
in the gazebo at the lawn party? I am
detecting a pattern in her behavior.
I am detecting I'm not in it. Why does
she dress like everybody else, and whose idea
was the hair? That was me, at the park,
drinking wine, struggling with a rhyme
for "orange," which she gave me but which
I forgot. I'm in the middle of my life.
It's high time she proves she loves me
best of all. I'd forgive her if she would.
Now, Muse, just tell me, what do I have
to say for myself? Don't leave me hanging
till next Friday, when the exact middle of my life
is scheduled to come back around.

Poem in which Orpheus rearranges the world yet again:

All day long the mountains
kept falling down at his feet.
All day long he put them back up,
rehanging the clouds for Hollywood special effect,
far as the eye could see uprooting the solitary trees,
answering their informal requests, for no fee at all,
to stand in a pleasant grove.

When he appealed to his flute,
commensurate with his responsibility,
the avalanche was quickly arrested,
the hurricane subsided, having no better idea.

So why now, here in his room, the garden,
snacking on olives, does he recall
that woman he couldn't turn his back on,
and hum a tune, putting the whole world naturally
to sleep, not in his personal darkness but in its own
            continuing light?

Now nothing to look forward to—except for that dream
of being torn in every imaginable direction.
And the mail from his admirers stacked up in the corner
and tomorrow more benefits for the underground.

Poem in which he depends upon a passing familiarity with baseball and the works of Sir Walter Scott:

Marchetti could not hit the ball that far.
But then he did. I don't know. I do not know.
A pitch that hung out over the letters? a tipped-off change-up?
a batting-practice fastball across the fat white heart of the plate?
From right field I couldn't really be sure of anything—
except Marchetti had somehow hit a home run and we'd lost
another game.
                          Sir Walter Scott had a different idea.

We called the center fielder Sir Walter Scott.
He wore a shiny suit to the school dances,
he was the only one to get through *Ivanhoe*
with his eyes wide open at the end.
On the school bus to the games, where the pro scouts
wrote him up, he'd just stare out the window,
intent on something most of us couldn't contemplate.
"Willie Scott's bat and glove do the talking," said the papers.

So when Marchetti connected, Sir Walter Scott took off,
refusing to accept the obvious, turning his back to the plate,
throwing himself at last up against the top of the fence.
                          It sounded like a transmission
dropping to the street, like gears grinding.
And his body seemed to gather itself up in mid-air
before it fell down in slow double and triple folds,
like a dress did in our collective fantasies,
like hedge-clippings on a hot Saturday afternoon,
like a movie pirate's doubloons glinting in the sun
while Marchetti kept circling the bases
as if it mattered, and the ball came to rest
in the mucid javelin pit. In a few years, a body bag
would remove Willie from another field.

Playing ball with my son today on the same field,
catching my breath on the warning track,
minty explosions of cut grass in the air,
the same eucalyptus trees shedding their bark
and straining like us to free themselves of the earth,
I turned for one last time, hoping now
Marchetti would be thrown out at the plate,
and found myself running and standing still all at once,
toward Walter Scott there on the grassy meads,
tilting forever in his shimmering mail, as if
baseball were played as it should be in the clouds.

IV

Poem in which he faces a firing squad after weeks of reading Latin American fiction:

When geese scatter and dogs
on porches wake with
a start and conversations in
the square come to a halt and
children suddenly abandon
their games and while bullets
hang suspended in midair
as leaves do when
they drop and seem to
be conflicted by wind
blindfolded from what
I failed to notice anyway in
the end unable to say the right thing
to those I wished to love
about the eclipsing beast's
countenance glued to the inside
of my reflection and on the leaf
I would inscribe the story of
my life while somewhere the leaf drifts
down in a wood I have never known
and the hummingbird shoots up
in dust lit gold as I pass this time
across unfallen leaves on a walk
that I plan on dreaming
does not ever stop.

Poem in which the concept of *closure* is addressed:

Bitter pill, closure.
Astronaut food, a sandwich of wonder bread.
Cinders in the salad, bonfires of toothpicks.
When did the madman pick all the locks?
Where's your sherpa when you need one?
You know once you get the bumblebees talking
they are impossible to stop. They want us to taste
their hunger, to introduce us to the queen
but who needs a queen? Some places I never leave
are places I've never been. Take that turret
for instance, and a certain princess whose braids
tumble down for me to clamber up.
I am thinking of the ocean floor, making change
for a gold doubloon and the treasure of the casket
jammed with old photographs. When I stood
on the veld there was the stampede of zebra,
which I also could not leave. There are docks
and there are doorways where I can still be found
going over the mail and the misery of passing time.
You know how the night inks your eyes clear
of light and you're the last one off the carousel?
You know when you spin a globe and stop it
with your thumb in the middle of Mozambique?
That's me, striding along, a wily baritone,
a snake jar on my head, but some places,
say alongside you, never come round again.
The last place I wrote you was the Sierra retreat.
As before the potbelly stove was overrun with ants.
At sunset the deer came down for a good drink.
The piano stood upright and tragic after the quake
that littered the field with bric-a-brac and closure.
Bees, be quiet for once. Sun, stay glued to my face.

Poem in which he posits several inevitabilities:

He thought the Tragic Muse sneezed in his ear on
The Fourth of July, but it was just a brass oom-pah-pah
band oom-pah-pah in the Tuileries oom-pah-pah.
Whenever he's at a loss, he makes a fancy allusion.
Seems that Roger Maris, year after he hit sixty-one,
ate nothing but escargots. For real. Then McGwire
went for seventy. Only in gauze-gowned retrospect seems it
inevitable. When he spies a bovinian Constable,
surrender he must to a bucolic urge and take a good
walking stick and a crew of border collies back to
the mother ship. Oh, amours of loony selenographers.
It's not impossible, to have had another life.
The trick is to live free of epistemological presuppositions
and a totalitarian country with state-sponsored terrorism.
Now, when he hears the cockroaches' wings—
that's a bad omen for party guests who won't leave
and need the bathroom yet again and it puts a crimp
in his postprandial designs with the one whose voice
makes him feel itchy inside and under his scalp.
Damn roaches. They will inherit the earth, which
is 90% bacteria, though after final faculty evaluations
he would have guessed more. Some nights are long ones
that's for sure, when he can't quite sleep or stay
awake, and he eats a bowl of cereal in company with TV.
One time it was *Othello*, and there was no time to lose.
The general will wobble off again, and he will orate
his life away to the late-arriving impotentates.
Something's a little bit wrong with his imagination, too,
the way it sets him up for disappointment and not just
on summer vacation, but he can't change even a little
his wish to change just a little, not to mention the moue
of a Constable, a damsel, and a killer with a quick delivery.

Poem in which he addresses some problems with fathers:

Besides mortality, let's not ignore the superventions du jour.
How many brain cells bite it on the way to morning
while you uncap a bottle and count off the stars?
I digress, but. What happened and what was made up
and what's the difference? Was there a puppy? Did you play
catch till the sun winked above the, I don't know, *oak tree?*
You're pretty sure you didn't go to *Turandot* or flip off
a manta ray at H_2O *World.* The combination you devise
for letting somebody know you were in love. Trouble
with fathers is that the lake sloshes against the endless wharf,
and you can't get over how shark skin feels so much like
his chin stubble, and when you change the oil in the car
you watch him pass down the street into another life.
Trouble with fathers is the trouble with, could be, me.
A twig that snaps underneath my boots in darker woods.
Rifle report that stops mid-echo a caw from completion.
The trouble with fathers has to do with fingerprints
on the windowsill of your old room, where you climbed in
after a night of practicing how to switch gears,
play defense with your feet, keep your eyes open
when taking a punch, roast black a red pepper and put
it inside a paper bag to sweat, tie a Windsor knot,
negotiate a mortgage and a plot with a prime bay view,
take care of your mother, take care, care, care, care.

Poem in which angels see what they see at twilight:

*"[Augustine] called 'morning knowledge' the angels' knowledge
of things in their primordial being...and 'evening knowledge'
their knowledge of created reality..."*

Aquinas

At water's edge of wire-service photographs
snapped in the aftermath of twisters, quakes, floods,
and forest fires, count on seeing the dogs. Sometimes
they prance through devastation on leashes,
sometimes they stare out from newsprint, beg for bone
or tennis ball to be thrown. You see them dig through
rubble, seeking out anybody's besotted love.
The world is overrun with angels, but twilight ones,
since that's our sort of world. That's what makes a hawk
miss a lucky field mouse. Hand it to them, though,
they're busy, the twilight angels, cuing up
migrations of endangered birds and butterflies,
rearranging sand castles, losing receipts and reasons
to live, getting hung up inside the silo or the wine bin.
They're turning up the volume in the storm, telling you
it's closing time, whittling the telephone poles into
pencils, holding up the day's final ski lift for you to ascend.
They whisper, Gaze back into the stranger's eyes one
second more. They are good with your friend's money
and bad with sympathy cards, loose with praise
and tight with advice. They have little stake in keeping
your marriage or integrity intact, so that's why
they're doing check-out in the express line,
chalking up the victim on the sun-pliant asphalt.
They won't hurry you out of the salon once the brawl's
in full swing. And then when you make your grand
entrance with the headless horse, they erase the words
you memorized and grant redundant permission

to sing an unscripted ditty, dance a tarantella.
That's what they do best, the twilight angels,
they wander deserts because they know how
the movie has to end and won't tell you why.
And after high tide traps the scout troop inside the sea
cave, starfish intumesce on the xanthic shore.
The angels seed the rainy roads from a basket of ball bearings.
They take up residence in your vacated rooms,
they answer breathlessly the phone when you're gone
and promise to write down a message if they find a pen.

Poem in which he corrects at the press conference the erroneous news reports:

I caught, OK, this morning morning's minion,
surgically implanted the chirp and the micro-chip,
and unlatched the mnemonic cage. Also, that shoplifting charge
was dismissed when I proved those seraphic-choir
robes were destined eventually to be mine. I am not in fact
an only child and I was technically never adopted once
in my life. Hirsute and bejeweled denizens of
The Fourth Estate, be informed it was I who fomented
riots in the hibernaculum over my self-imposed production
         quotas,
I who organized demonstrations of anthropomorphic animals
against myself and my spavinizing farm policies.
My taxes and milk cartons are what you'd call current,
I am bullish on the matador market, never sucked
on metal I did not find precious, and the inside-
trader info pertaining to self-ironing chinos con tequila
will not be traced back to me. Now, as for those compromising
photographs I posed for when I was an undergrad
cosmology student in need of rent money, I want
you to know the legumes were not my idea.
I did marry seven times, but all to the same woman,
and as the mopey liar and dyslexic Heraclitus once opined,
you cannot really step into the same residue twice—
not that any red-blooded American won't mostly try.
Beyond that, my spiritual inclinations are nobody's biz
but Jesus', and I take no credit for discovering the Internet,
foreshadowing, cambozola cheese, or the Pythagorean theorem.
So you want dirty linen? You like a skeleton in the closet?
All right. Once I found solace in a Cancun cabana,
but the cerveza was cold and the slippery sea had pulled
the murky curtain down on the estivating matinee,
if I may be so bold as to ask you to butt out.
I spilled a pint of my own blood on the files,

but only because I could not get her to budge.
Soon after I was the first astronaut in space blessed
with acrophobia, tenure, and a mild case of the mange,
but I have since resettled on terra firma,
two-thirds in love with easeful gravitas.
I did unmoor the heiress's balcony rail
though not for those reasons ruthfully alleged.
I'm stuck on an old desire to navigate a cloud,
to coruscate competitively with a chandelier,
I'm stuck, which I want to make perfectly clear.
I want to inoperate the formerly operative assertions.
Success will never go to my head. Murals are on mirrors,
my eyes shaded with trompe l'oeil tape, all of the above
opted for on the standardized examinations.
Finally, when spring roisters about who does not feel
anxious as a man on the brink of executive clemency?
That's when flying buttresses take wing. I've always
placed my faith in the kindness, you know, of swimmers,
how they let me flail and flop in the fast lane
of the lap pool. My favorite color is a shadow
beamed by a tocsin moon. As you asked me to do,
I have reviewed my notes and the video.
I never actually claimed I was going to live forever.

Poem in which an escape takes place:

Each day carries an alias, an airtight alibi,
a great scheme to get rich or free quick.
I drive the getaway car and my fingerprints
litter the paths of my escape like the ashes
of burnt banknotes and stolen securities,
the only kind in the world I could acquire.
So in the end, who would not squeeze the trigger,
sign someone else's flamboyant name, light
the bomb and run?
                    Crossing state lines, into Kansas,
watching the exodus of blackbirds from the snapping
wires, who would not look up and see, somewhere
in the distance, El Dorado, Elysium, Oz, California?

Poem in which he has trouble with this elegy for Bathsheba's first husband, Uriah, a loyal soldier whose death in war was neatly arranged by King David, who would become her second:

But hold on, not so fast,
let's not get started, otherwise
there would be the Absalom Absalom
stuff memorialized by Faulkner
—and a son's death due to a
father's folly is too much pain,
then and now, to recount,
or the business with Achitophel,
famous advisor, Kissinger-prototype,
or the matter of unfortunate, beautiful
Tamar, raped by one brother
revenged by another.
(But the worst part for her was how
Amnon loathed her after,
how he turned her out bolting his door,
how she wept and rent her
virgin's robes and cast ashes on her head...)
Let the family chroniclers all
make clear, how the nation
watched like sleepy spectators
at a summertime air show
thrilled by a dazzling daredevil
stunt that suddenly left them killed.

Because all I wanted to do was
write an elegy for Uriah, the Hittite.
I don't think much about Hittites
normally but Browning was on my mind
and my poem began, like this:
"In the springtime of the year,
the time when kings go off to battle..."

but then I realized those lines
were already in Second Samuel,
which is, isn't it, always the way,
and besides, I couldn't work in when
David instructed Joab, "Send me Uriah,
the Hittite."
                              (This line is very ominous,
right out of *The Godfather*, not the book
either, because what David intends
to do is kill Uriah, after having spied
on Bathsheba, the wife, as she bathed
on the roof next door, and having
summoned her to his royal quarters,
where in no Biblical time at all,
pretty much conveniently offstage
they apparently fell in love.
I find "Send me Uriah, the Hittite"
the second or third saddest line
ever, right after "Tell Michael it was
nothing personal"—*Godfather* again—or
Browning's Porphyria's Lover, who says
sweetly, absently, "I found a thing to do,"
referring to winding the hair three times
around the neck of a rich woman he loves
but cannot do anything short of
a fairly serious murder to keep.)

But along about this time, I grew
wary, convinced I would have to bring in
too much explanatory background
(unless the elegy got into the Norton,
and I could use my own footnotes...).
In any case, I would have to make clear
how David needed to seduce Uriah himself,
by making him, fresh and bloodied
from the battle with the Ammonites

(another people like us lost in time),
report to his own house and wash his feet
(David's strict and probably altogether
unpeculiar instruction for the time)
so that the king could make a credible case
that the baby who would someday be born
to Bathsheba could just possibly be
Uriah's own. Why, David even poured
the good stuff to get the soldier in the mood.
But today who would not suspect this ploy?
And here's the most curious part of all:
Uriah, loyal Uriah, who routinely risked
his life for David on the battlefield,
tonight would defy his king.
He left David's holy presence and camped
all night outside the booths that housed
the ark of the covenant instead
and slept with his soldiers
and never went to Bathsheba's (euphemistic)
side.

      When David found out next morning,
he knew a man this clever or this pure
or this dumb must be killed,
which authorities have always known,
and this is when he said, "Send me..." etc.,
though I bet there's some scroll from
the Dead Sea that goes into greater detail,
with David saying, "He did what...?"
All we know for sure is that now
Joab summarily isolated Uriah
in the fray and allowed him to be killed
by a stone an Ammonite woman flung
from the besieged walls of Rabbah,
and David's communications office could
maintain conveniently a posture
of plausible, upright deniability.

Maybe I should have, speaking of
Browning, written it from Uriah's
pathetic point of view—but that's the whole
problem, I don't think the man had one,
a distinct point of view. Sometimes love
destroys a man's imagination, and
sometimes it's the other way around.
Uriah simply saw what he could see,
Uriah did what he could do—and that's
the mystery of betrayals like this:
they're so ordinary, utterly.
The betrayed is betrayed first of all
by the essential fact he is incidental.
And my theory is that, like all
the betrayed, Uriah always always knew.
(People had been stopping him
in Jerusalem, shocked by his sallow
face, asking what happened to his sense
of humor, asking what's wrong,
as he stumbled against the wells
and talked to himself
and blanched at their questions
as to how was Bathsheba and
when should they block out time
for an expected invitation to a bris.
He had tsuris before he could
explain why. In another age, he might
have joined a support group, got a
good lawyer, written essays,
taken up tai chi, aerobics, dope, or gin.)
That last night he refused to go home
and look into the eyes of Bathsheba,
his wife who'd have to lie.
That last night I figure he barely slept

and readied himself to accommodate
David's and Bathsheba's and God's holy will.
It doesn't matter much I suppose, since
Uriah's case was lost since his first date
with the daughter of Eliam, he was a goner
from the first time Bathsheba stroked
his beard, he was expendable from the time
he was recruited for David's elite.
So when David sent for him,
Uriah simply went, understanding if not
knowing that he was already dead
for about three thousand years
and that desire is a terrible, terrible
thing for a man who is not involved
and that murder and desire for another man's
wife are absolutely intertwined.
If you don't believe Uriah or this poem,
there's a book he and I would recommend.

Poem in which he writes the last poem in which:

The summer death's terror
was casually displaced,
the old dog we loved took
to walking into closed doors,
standing in the sun, staring
with eyes' spooling into space.
Then she'd burrow into sleep
as if sleep were a cave where
the interesting bones were hid.
Later, she'd turn from her bowl
and listen to hovering bees.
We placed her under the shade
between our two maple trees.
Whole centuries believed.
And still the old news stuns
when the phone rings,
the middle of the night.
Our voices are the ones that break.
We dress ourselves in the dark.
We're driving somewhere before we think.

Poem in which a vision is recalled:

We were thirty rungs high in the chapel tower
while the country conducted a religious war.
That night, we had a vision—of Jack Daniels.
And revealed before us was The Miracle of
the Cracked Ice. Still, something more—or something
else—surged with us past the midnight rooms,
compelled us through the white gold chapel,
hopelessly lifting us up the creaky ladder to
the top of the spire that none of us risked ascending before.
In grape-crushing time, catching our breath
in the resinous, chewy breeze coming off the lake,
we remarked on the high beams heading for town.

From up there, I saw the deer finesse
the vines with tenuous, postoperative tenderness.
And probably the night probably passed. Then
something like a tide reversed, and something
like shooting stars differently fell,
and something like rumors confused all the trees.
Here I was, close to heaven as I'd ever be,
a citizen of the next and a stranger in this
and in all worlds to be redeemed.

ABOUT THE AUTHOR

Joseph Di Prisco has published poems, essays, and reviews in numerous journals, and his first book, *Wit's End,* was published by the University of Missouri Press. He was awarded The Young Poets and The Theodore Roethke Prizes from *Poetry Northwest.* He taught for over twenty years, middle school, high school, and college, and he is co-author of a book about adolescence and growing up, *Field Guide to the American Teenager,* published by Perseus Books. His novel, *Confessions of Brother Eli,* will be published in Fall 2000 by MacAdam/Cage. His web site is www.diprisco.com. He was born in New York City and now lives in Berkeley, California, with his wife, photographer Patricia James, and their three supportive dogs.